Floella's
Cardboard
Book

Cardboard boxes can be as much fun as expensive toys – if you know how to make the most of them. Popular TV presenter, Floella Benjamin, has put together a fantastic collection of fun ideas using cardboard boxes, a few simple tools and heaps of imagination!

Illustrated by Chris Evans

*Also by Floella Benjamin
in Magnet Books*

Floella's Fun Book
Floella's Fabulous Bright Ideas Book

Floella's **Cardboard Box** Book

Floella Benjamin

A Magnet Book

First published in 1987 as a Magnet paperback original
by Methuen Children's Books Ltd
11 New Fetter Lane, London EC4P 4EE
Text copyright © 1987 Floella Benjamin
Illustrations copyright © 1987 Chris Evans
Printed in Great Britain
by Richard Clay Ltd, Bungay, Suffolk

British Library in Publication Data

Benjamin, Floella
  Floella's cardboard box book. –
  (A Magnet book).
  1. Handicraft – Juvenile literature
  I. Title
  145.5   TT160

  ISBN 0-416-04442-5

This paperback is sold subject to the condition
that it shall not, by way of trade or otherwise,
be lent, re-sold, hired out or otherwise circulated
without the publisher's prior consent in any
form of binding or cover other than that in which
it is published and without a similar condition
including this condition being imposed
on the subsequent purchaser.

WHY FLOELLA'S CARDBOARD BOX BOOK?

I've heard it said many times that children seem to find the cardboard box the toy arrived in more entertaining than the toy itself! This is what prompted me to write *Floella's Cardboard Box Book*.

Cardboard boxes come in all shapes and sizes and with a few simple tools and a bit of ingenuity, you and your child can create interesting, exciting and cheap toys. Many of the items in the book are large enough to be sat on, in or even worn. My son Aston came up with many of the ideas for this book and they have been tried and tested on him and his friends. I'm sure you and your children will want to add your own ideas and decorate or paint the boxes in your own creative way. So go ahead, enjoy yourselves and you might even start thinking up your own things to make out of cardboard boxes.

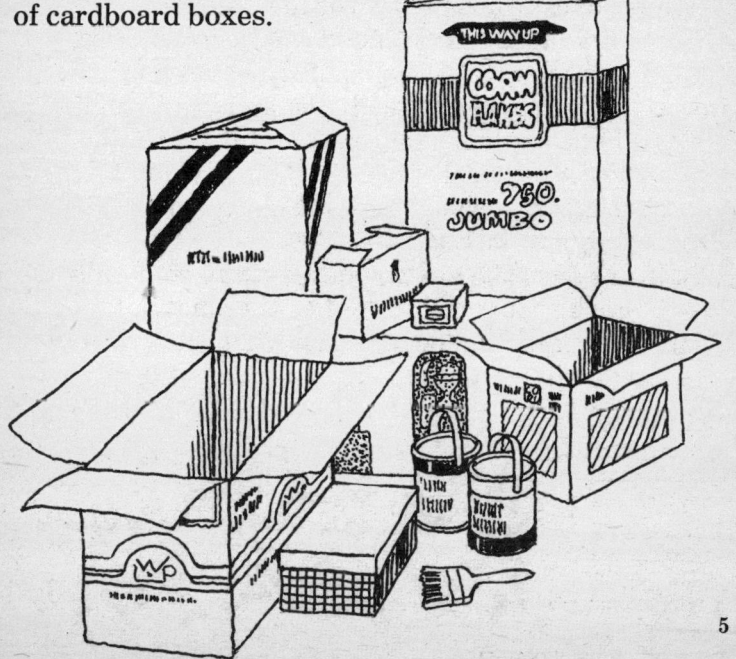

Where To Get Boxes

The easiest place to get boxes from is your local supermarket. Many stores put them by the checkout and are only too glad for you to take them away. I always load my shopping into one rather than a carrier bag. Some supermarkets, however, have decided that large unsightly piles of empty boxes don't go with their super glossy image and the boxes are efficiently crushed into neat bundles and thrown away. What a waste! If your supermarket is like this, it's worth asking one of the warehouse staff if they would mind saving two or three boxes from the jaws of the crusher.

For really large boxes a good source is electrical appliance stores. Televisions, microwaves and freezers come packed in really big and very tough boxes. If you explain what you want it for to the manager of your local store, they usually don't mind letting you collect one from the goods entrance round the back.

I always save the box whenever I buy something new. I stack them one inside the other and put them in the loft. You never know when they might come in handy.

What Tools Will You Need?

Scissors are definitely not the best way of cutting shapes out of a cardboard box. All you end up doing is getting blisters on your fingers from trying to force them through the tough cardboard. I find the best method is with a craft knife. The only problem with craft knives is that they are *very, very sharp*. If a toddler gets its hands on one there is no telling what might happen. So I have devised a safe way of using a craft knife. First of all I use the type that has a retractable blade, then I tie a string through the hole in the handle (most of them have one), then I tie the other end of the string round my belt and pop the knife in my pocket when I'm not using it.

This ensures that you can never accidentally put the knife down where tiny hands can get hold of it. In addition to the craft knife, I always have some sticky tape handy. The very wide brown parcel tape is best but ordinary sellotape will do. You'll need strong glue, too. The white woodworking adhesive is best and it isn't dangerous. A ruler, of course, and a pencil are essential, then felt tips, poster paints and brushes to finish off.

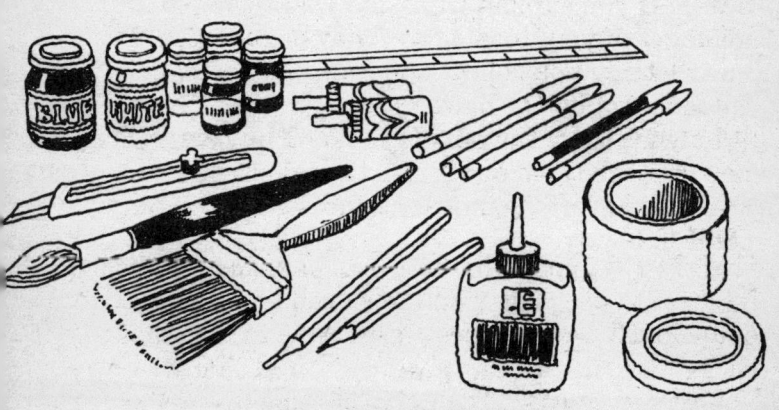

Extras
To make ideas come alive you will need Christmas wrapping paper and wallpaper, wallpaper paste, empty plastic bottles and containers, cardboard tubes – in fact any household bits and pieces that might come in useful.

Paint
I've always found whenever I'm painting cardboard it's best to use poster paint or even household emulsion. To get the best results make sure that the paint is as thick as possible. I find that watery paint takes ages to dry and it also makes the cardboard soggy and the box will tend to dry warped.

Corrugations
When cutting cardboard a useful tip is to cut along the corrugations if possible, as it helps to give you a straight line. You will also find it's much easier to bend the cardboard along the corrugations, so bear that in mind before you start to cut the box up.

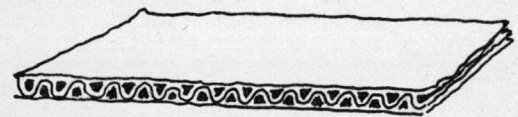

Measurements
The ideas in this book are meant to be simple and quick to make so I don't want to complicate things with lots of confusing measurements. As cardboard boxes come in all different shapes and sizes I've tried to keep exact measurements to a minimum. The drawings and diagrams should give a pretty good idea of the shape of the box required for each item and how it should look when it's finished.

Grading System
Here's a quick guide to all the ideas in the book. You can begin with the simple ones and work your way up to the most challenging.

☆ Quick and simple to make

	page
Breakfast in bed tray stand	16
Bus	18
Crazy Golf	22
Dried Flower Vase	32
Giant Dice	34
Hats	36
Kennel	38
Pet's Basket	44
Postbox	52
Table	70
Television	71

☆☆ Bit more difficult and time-consuming

Aquarium	12
Desk Tidy	24
Dolls' Pram	30
Picnic Basket	46
Service Station	57
Ship	59
Sofa	62
Space Station	64
Space Suit	66
Suitcase	68
Train	72
Washing Machine	74

☆ ☆ ☆ Quite difficult but very rewarding

Birdcage	14
Car	20
Dolls' House	26
Marble Game	40
Periscope	42
Pinball Machine	48
Punch & Judy Puppet Theatre	54
Wendy House	76

Have lots of fun!

AQUARIUM

Children find aquariums fascinating but real fish tanks are not always a practical proposition. So I will show you how to make the next best thing!

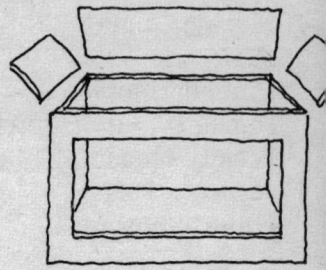

What You Need:
One oblong box; pebbles, rocks and shells; string; cling film; sticky tape; green crêpe paper; paint; coloured paper; blue tack.

What You Do:
1. Trim the flaps off the box then cut a rectangle out of one of the long sides, leaving about 4cm round the edge.

2. Paint the inside walls of the box greeny blue and the floor sandy yellow.

3. When the paint is dry, tape a piece of cling film inside the front and stretch it across the opening.
4. Now arrange the pebbles and shells on the sandy bottom of the aquarium using blue tack to hold them in place.

5. Cut six pieces of string just long enough to go across the top of the box and tape them in place.
6. Tear thin strips of crêpe paper and hang them over the strings.

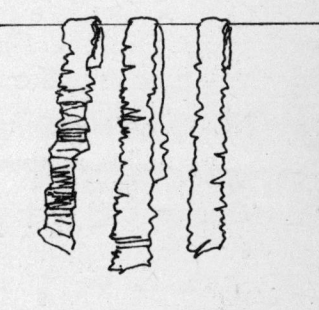

7. Cut fish shapes from the coloured paper and tape them to different lengths of string. Then hang them inside the aquarium.
8. Finally cover the aquarium with a cardboard lid.

You will be amazed how real the aquarium looks.

BIRDCAGE

Here is an easy-to-make bird cage. It's not meant to keep a real bird in but it looks very pretty hanging up with a toy bird inside.

What You Need:
One small box, about 20cm square; 32 thin plastic drinking straws; one wire coathanger; white paint; strong glue; a pair of pliers (the type with a bit for cutting wire); tape.

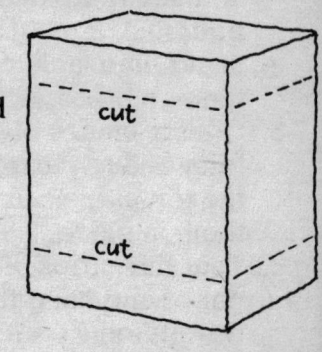

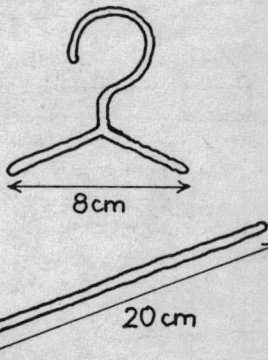

What You Do:
1. Cut the bottom and top off the box, leaving a 4cm lip all round. Make sure the corrugations are vertical. Cut a flap in the bottom of one of them just big enough to get your hand through.
2. Paint them white and leave to dry.
3. Use the pliers to cut up the coat hanger. You will need a 20cm length for the perch

and the hook part with about 4cm left either side of it. 
4. Pierce a hole in the centre of the box without the flap. Bend the ends of the hook straight, push it through the hole and tape in place. 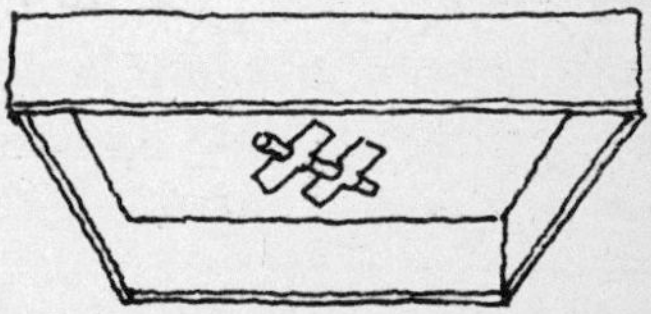
5. To make the perch, use the pliers to bend the 20cm length into a U shape and then bend the ends out at right angles. Pierce two holes either side of the hook and push the perch through.
6. Dip the end of each straw in the glue and push it into a corrugation on the base of the cage about 3cm apart. Start at one corner and work your way round.
7. When all the straws are in, dab some glue on the other ends and fit the top on the cage.
8. Place a toy bird on the perch and tape the flap shut.

Breakfast in bed tray stand

If you want to treat someone to breakfast in bed or if there's someone in your house who is poorly and has to have their meals in bed, here's a useful tray stand so they can eat in comfort.

What You Need:
One long shallow box; some scrap wallpaper (the vinyl type is perfect as it can be wiped clean); clear sticky tape; craft knife.

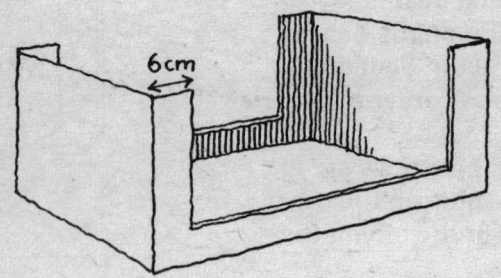

What You Do:
1. Trim the flaps off the box and cut a section out of both sides leaving about 6cm all round.
2. Cover with fancy paper held in place with sticky tape.

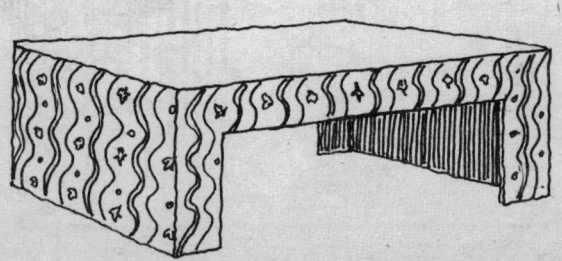

17

This little bus is great for giving teddy bears and dolls a ride. It's simple and quick to make and it's useful for storing toys in when they are not being played with.

What You Need:
One large box; one small box; red paint; sticky tape; glue.

What You Do:
1. Round off the corners of the flaps on the large box and tape them upright.
2. Cut four windows in each side and two windows in each end.

3. Glue the small box below the window on the front of the bus.
4. Paint some wheels and a radiator grill on and finish the bus off in bright red paint.

Fill up the bus with teddies and dolls and hold tight!

CAR

Here's how to make a car that looks as good as anything you see on the roads.

What You Need:
One very large box; one small box; silver foil.

What You Do:
1. Trim the flaps off the box and then mark out the wheels on each side. Use a large saucepan lid as a guide.

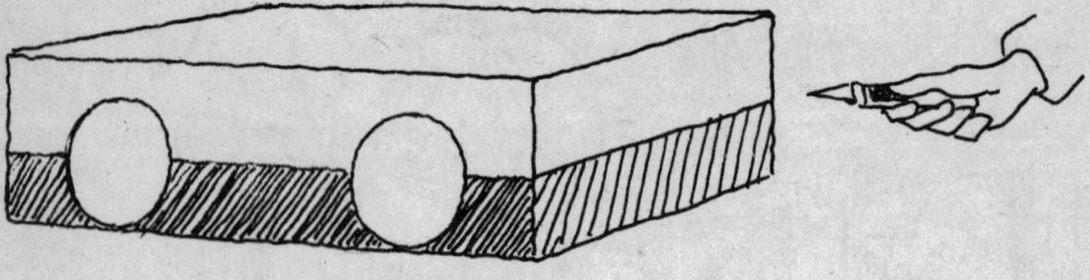

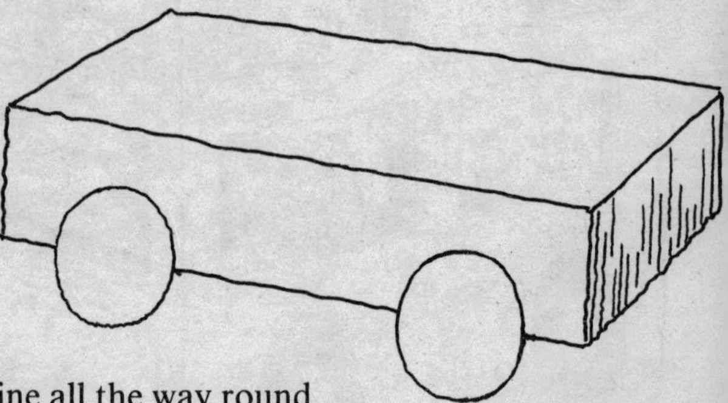

2. Mark a line all the way round the box half-way up the wheels.
3. Cut round the line.
4. Follow the diagram and mark out lines for the boot, the bonnet and the windscreen and seat back.

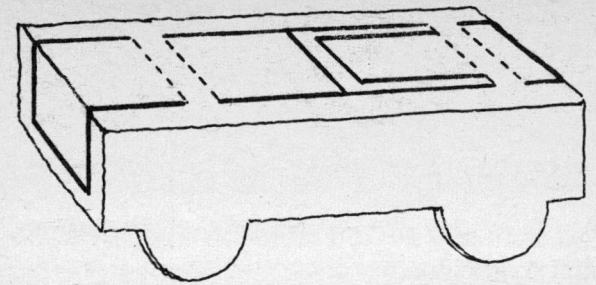

5. Fold the windscreen up and the seat back down.
6. Cut four 10cm circles from the foil for headlights and hubcaps.
7. Stick the foil headlights on the front, paint the tyres black and stick foil hubcaps on the wheels.
8. Place the small box inside to sit on.

CRAZY GOLF

This is a fun game that can be played inside or out.

What You Need:
Four medium sized boxes; wide parcel tape; two plastic lemonade bottles; four empty margarine containers; paint and brushes.

What You Do:
You will need four holes on this crazy golf course. Each one is made the same way. Just paint them different colours and number them one to four.
1. Trim the flaps off the box and cut out one side.
2. Cut a hole about 8cm in diameter half-way down the opposite side.
3. Use the side you've cut out as a slope by taping it inside the box at an angle.

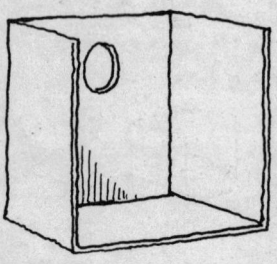 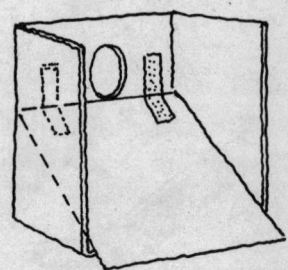

4. Cut the plastic bottles in half and then cut the top and bottom off.
5. Tape one section of the plastic bottle to the back of the box underneath the hole.

6. Make the other three crazy golf holes the same way and lay out the course. Place a margarine container underneath each hole. Use a tennis ball and a stick to play crazy golf. The player must get the ball into the margarine containers to score a point.

DESK TIDY

This is a good way to keep all those pencils and paint brushes, erasers, pencil sharpeners and paper clips in one place.

What You Need:
One small box, a tissue box will do; three kitchen roll tubes; scraps of coloured wrapping paper; coloured stick-on shapes; glue; paint; sticky tape.

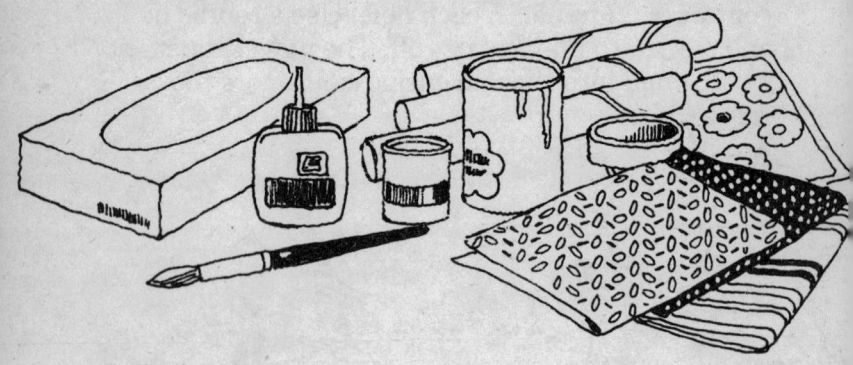

What You Do:
1. Trim the box to make a shallow tray about 5cm high.
2. Paint the tray a bright colour inside and out, and leave to dry.

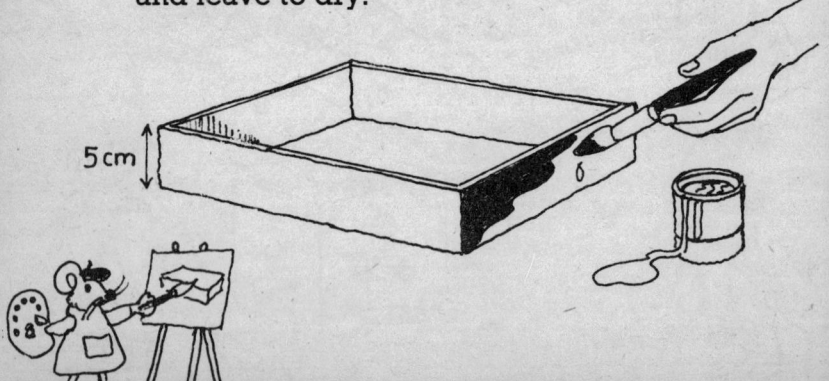

3. Cut the tubes into different lengths starting with a short one about 7cm long and going up to a long one about 16cm long. Paint them or cover them with wrapping paper. Decorate the tubes with sticky shapes or bits of coloured foil.
4. Glue the tubes securely inside the box. Fill it up with pens and pencils.

Dolls House

Whenever children see those beautiful Victorian dolls' houses they always say "I wish I could have one". Of course, the real ones are very expensive. Well don't despair because with a bit of ingenuity you can help your children to make their very own dolls' house. Here's how.

What You Need:
One large square box; glue; wallpaper paste; an assortment of scrap wallpaper, preferaby ones with small flowery patterns; scraps of lino, carpet and material; cling film.

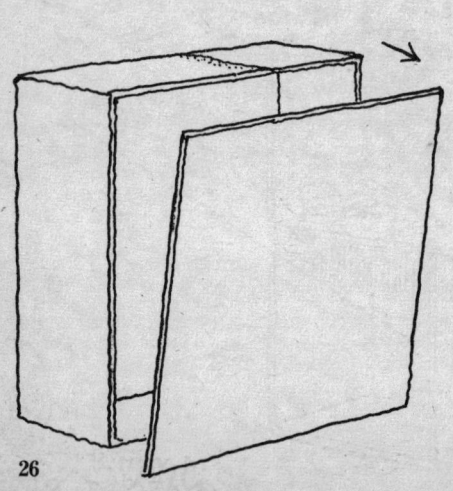

What You Do:
1. Tape the flaps closed on the box and then remove the whole of one side.
2. Cut the side in half, then mark a line in the centre

of each piece. Carefully cut half-way along the line on each of the pieces and fit them together as shown.

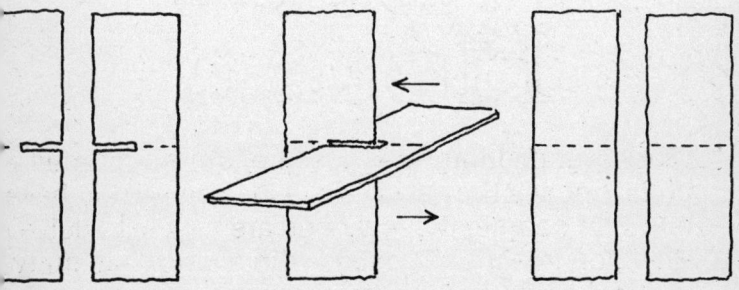

3. Fit the assembled piece inside the box and secure in place with tape.
4. Fold a piece of card to make a roof.

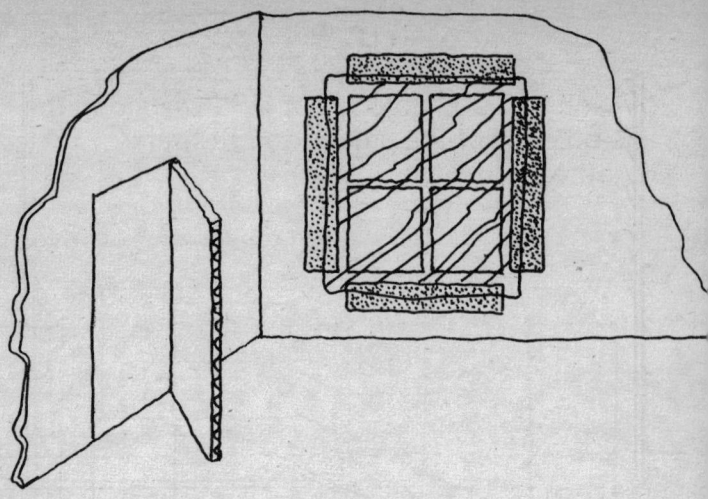

5. Cut out some windows and a door. Make the windows look as if they have glass in them by taping cling film across them.
6. Mix up the wallpaper paste and decorate the rooms. Use a pretty flowery paper for the upstairs bedrooms and perhaps a striped one for the living room downstairs. You could paint the kitchen walls a bright colour instead of wallpapering it. It's up to you, just like decorating a real house.
7. Cover the floors with carpet and stick lino in the kitchen.
8. Now you can use all your imagination to furnish the house using small boxes as table and chairs. Use bits of material stuck in place as curtains and tablecloths.

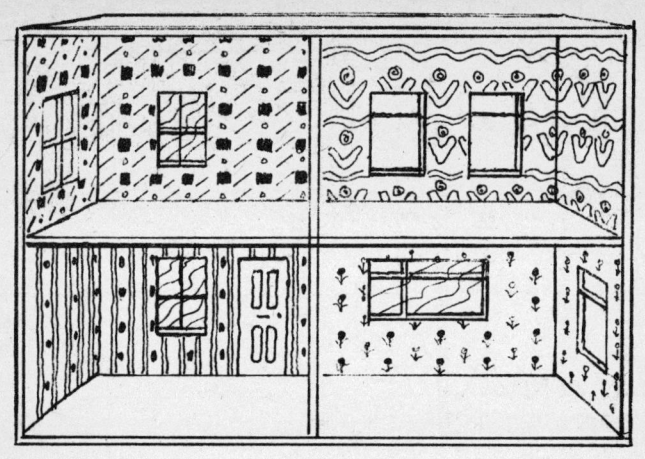

DOLLS PRAM

You will be amazed how simple it is to make this dolls' pram. Now all the toys can go for a ride.

What You Need:
Two boxes, one large and one small; four clothes pegs, the old fashioned wooden type that don't have springs; two pieces of 6mm dowel, or thin bamboo cane, about 5cm longer than the width of the smaller of the two boxes; parcel tape; a small plate; pencil; paint.

What You Do:
1. Close up the flaps on the smaller box and tape shut. Cut out the sections as shown in the picture.

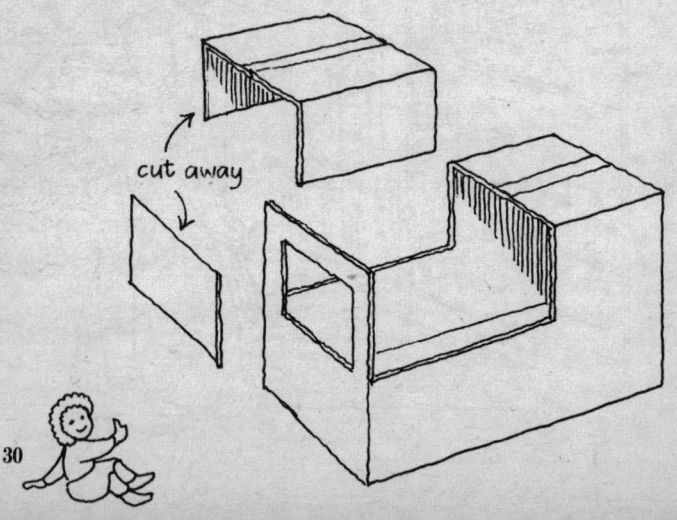

2. On the large box draw round a plate to make four wheels, cut them out, then use a pencil to pierce a small hole in the centre of each.
3. Pierce a hole with the pencil in each bottom corner of the pram.
4. Push a peg on to one end of a stick, slide on a wheel and push the stick right through the pram. Push the other wheel on and secure with another peg.

5. Paint the pram if you want and put some blankets and a pillow in it.

DRIED FLOWER VASE

What You Need:
One empty tissue box, the kind that is cube-shaped with a round hole at the top; glue; coloured paper; stick-on shapes or patterned wrapping paper; a couple of pebbles to weight the vase down and stop it toppling over when the flowers are placed in it.

What You Do:
1. Cover the box in coloured paper and decorate with stick-on shapes or use patterned wrapping paper instead.

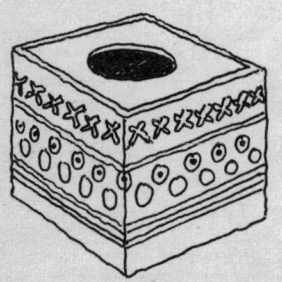 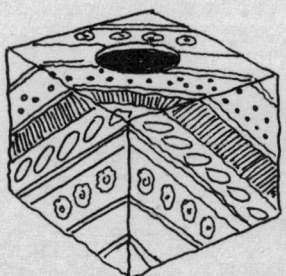

2. When the glue is dry, pop the pebbles in the vase then arrange some lovely dried flowers in it.

GIANT DICE

This dice is great to use for party games, indoors or out.

What You Need:
One square box; wallpaper paste; an old newspaper; black and white paint.

What You Do:
1. Close up the box and tape shut.
2. Mix up the wallpaper paste, making it very thick. Tear the newspaper into strips. Paste the newspaper all over the outside of the box. Make sure the strips go on in a criss cross pattern.

cover the box with strips of newspaper

3. Leave the box to dry, then give it a coat of white paint.

4. Finally, copy a real dice and paint on black dots from one to six.

HATS

Cardboard boxes can be used to make all sorts of hats. Here are a few ideas.

What You Need:
One small box just large enough to fit on your child's head; tape; crêpe paper; paint.

What You Do:

TOP HAT
Open up the flaps and then cut four small squares of cardboard to fit in the corners, tape them in place and paint the box. Make a hat band out of crêpe paper.

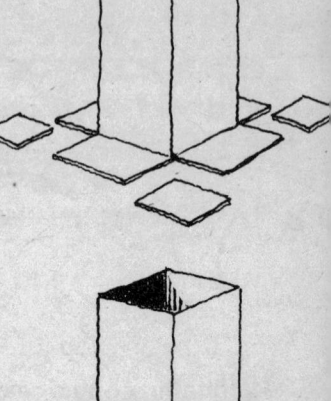

SOLDIER'S HAT
Cut off three of the flaps then trim the remaining one into a curved peak. Paint the hat bright red and the peak black. Use white or yellow crêpe paper as the hat band and a different colour for the plume.

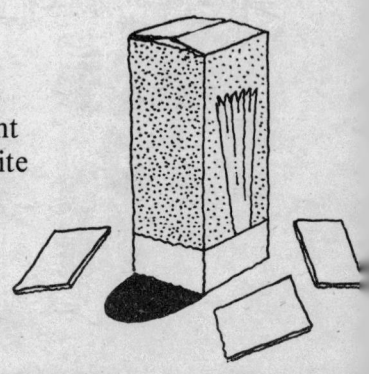

BOATER

1. You will need a larger box for this one. Measure round your child's head, then draw a circle roughly the same size on a large sheet of card cut from the side of the box.
2. Draw another circle about 16cm larger, round the outside of the first circle.
3. Cut a strip of card about 8cm wide and long enough to go round your child's head.
4. Cut out the small circle and keep the piece you remove, this makes the top of the hat.
5. Bend the long strip into a circle and tape the ends together.
6. Tape the top and the brim on, using plenty of tape.
7. Paint the hat and use black or brown crêpe paper as a hat band.

KENNEL

If you have a small puppy or toy dog then here is a home you can make for them.

What You Need:
Two large boxes, one slightly bigger than the other; craft knife; pencil; paint.

What You Do:
1. Trim the flaps off the smaller of the two boxes.
2. Mark out the doorway as shown in the drawing and cut it out.
3. To make the roof, mark and cut the slightly larger box as shown in the drawing, and glue it in place on top of the kennel.
4. Paint the kennel and leave to dry.
   Now watch your puppy snuggle up inside.

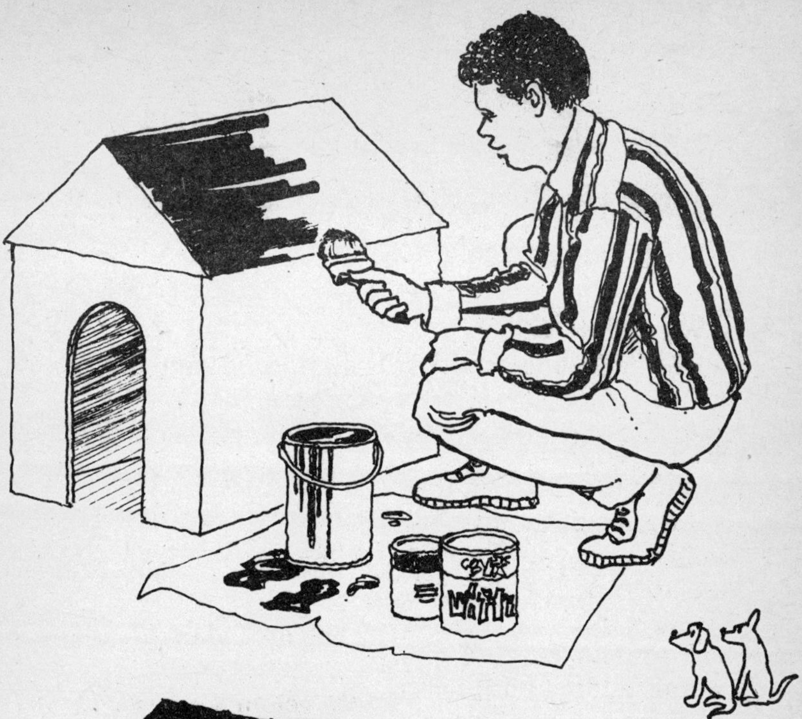

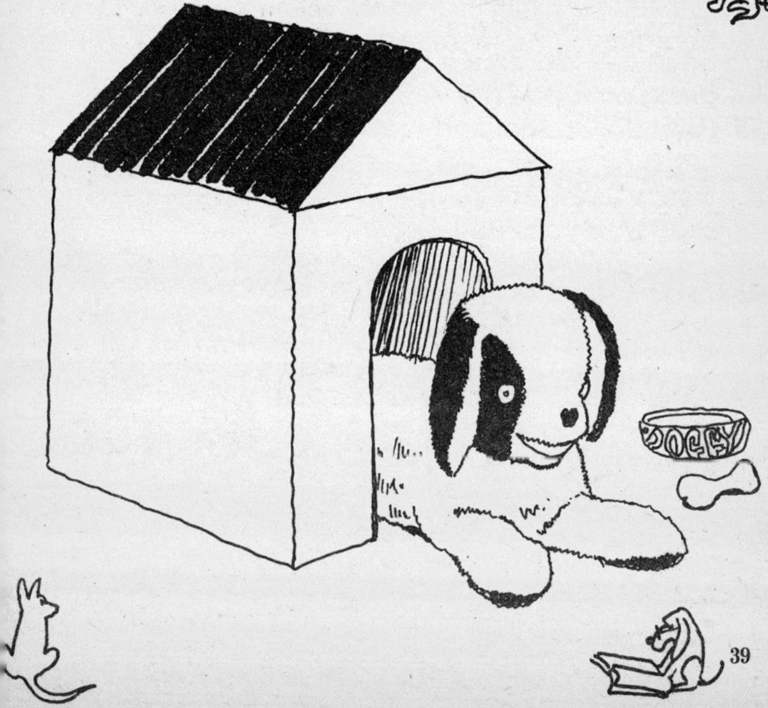
DOGGY

☆☆☆ MARBLE GAME

This is a fun puzzle that everyone will want a go at. You can make it easier, if you wish, for the tiny tots, or tougher for the big ones. Here's how.

What You Need:
One small box; paste; four marbles; a page of a magazine that has a full page picture on it. The picture can be of almost anything; I've used one of a teddy bear.

What You Do:
1. Cut a shallow tray from the side of the box. Make the edges about 4cm high.
2. Cut the other side of the box off and trim it so it fits neatly inside the tray without bending.
3. Paint the tray a nice bright colour.

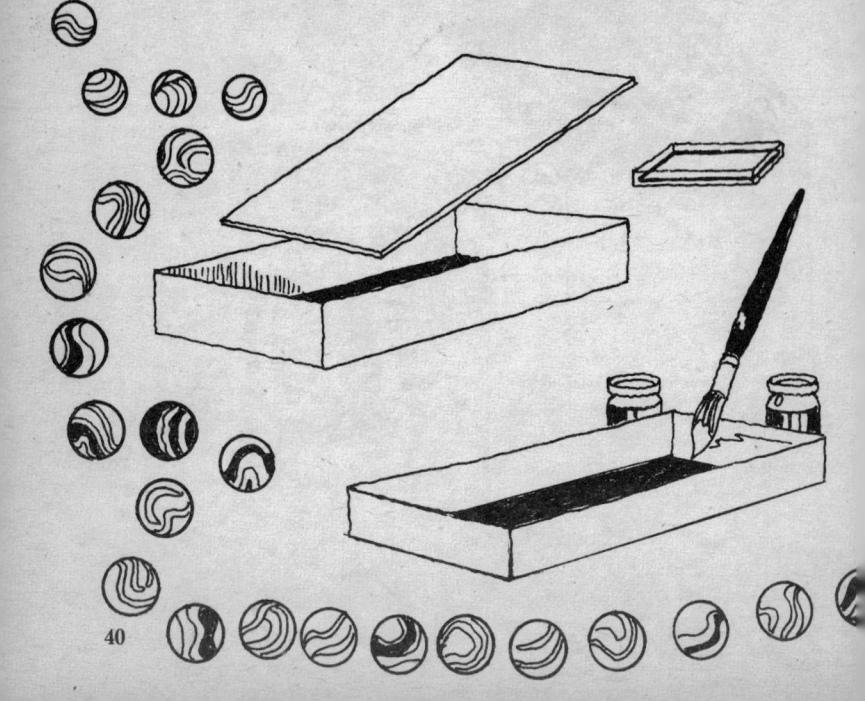

4. While the tray is drying, trim the picture so that it fits on the piece of cardboard and stick it down thoroughly.
5. Decide where the holes for the marbles will look best. I thought it looked good if the teddy bear in my picture was balancing one on each paw. When you have decided on each place, draw a circle round a five pence piece and cut a hole there with your craft knife.
6. Now glue the finished picture into the bottom of the tray and put the four marbles in. The idea of the game is to get all the marbles in the holes at the same time. It's not as easy as it looks! If you want the game to be harder, cut more holes and use more marbles.

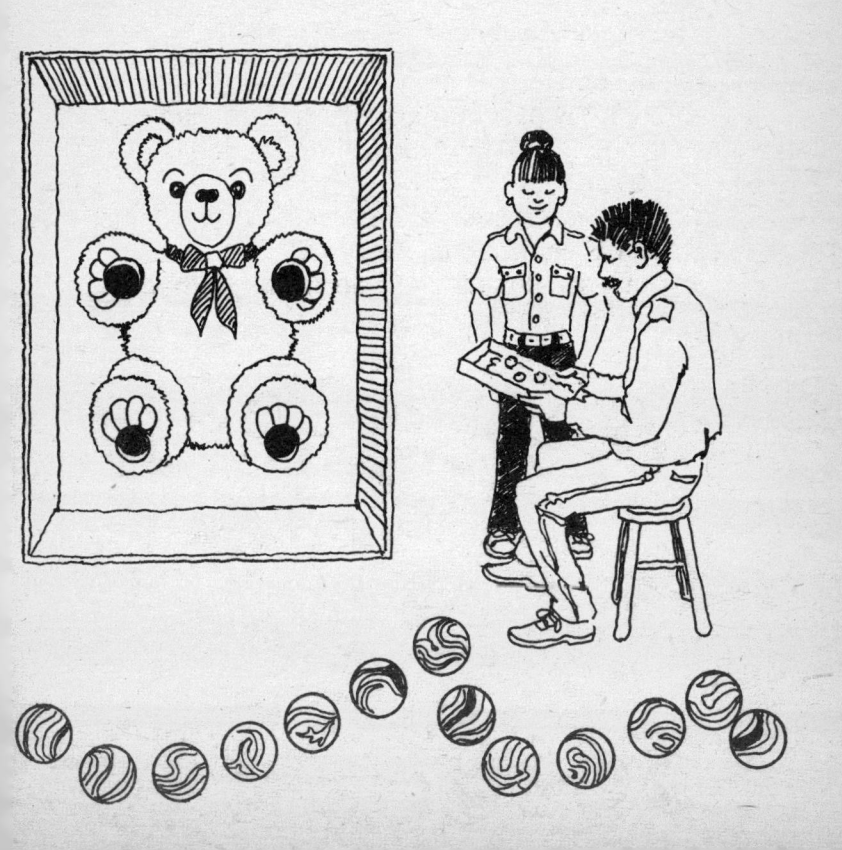

✰✰✰
PERISCOPE

If you have ever been to a crowded event where your children cannot see what's going on, then this simple periscope is the answer. Be careful with the mirrors, though. I suggest it's only used when there are adults around, just to be on the safe side. If you cannot find any old mirrors you can go to a glazier's shop and get them to cut you two small pieces just the right size.

What You Need:
One tall thin box; two mirrors, about 12cm square; strong sticky tape (carpet tape is ideal); a plastic 45° set square.

What You Do:
1. Cut a 12cm square out of the top of one side of the box. Turn the box over and do the same at the bottom.
2. With the set square, draw two 45° angle lines from the corners of the box.
3. Cut a slit along the 45° angle line so that the mirrors can slide in tightly.

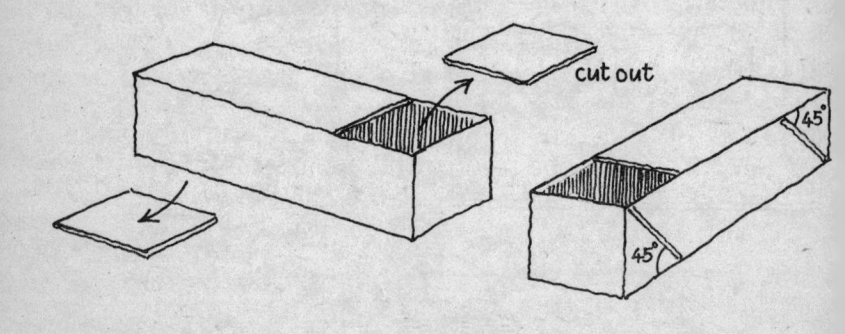

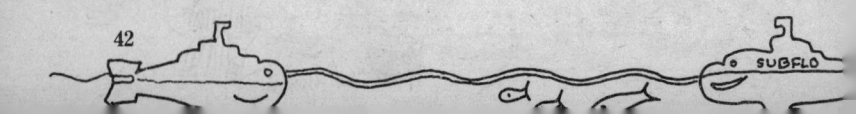

back of mirror

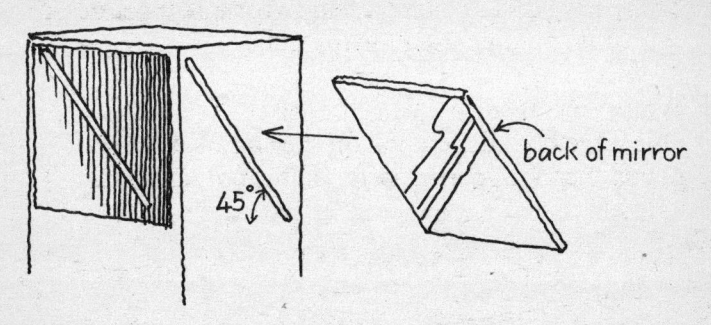

45°

4. Slide both mirrors into the slots, making sure the reflective surface of each is facing the right way. Then tape over the slots to stop the mirrors sliding out.

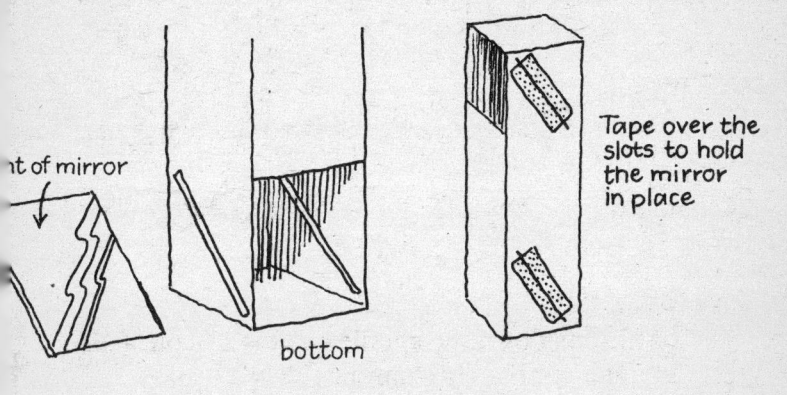

nt of mirror

Tape over the slots to hold the mirror in place

bottom

5. Paint the periscope if you want, and set off for the football match, parade or golf tournament.

PETS BASKET

This pet's basket could be handy for a real pet dog or cat, or it could be used for toy pets.

What You Need:
One large box (depending on the size of your pet); newspaper; wallpaper paste; paint; polyurethane varnish.

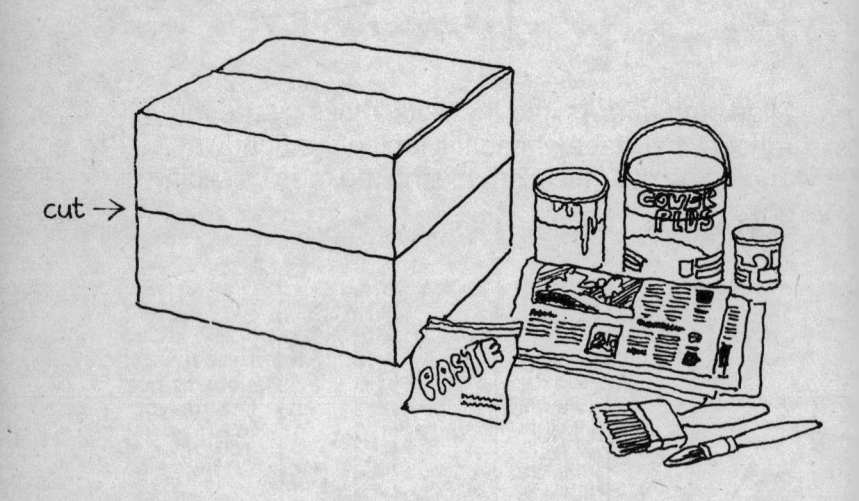

cut →

What You Do:
1. Cut the box down the middle and discard one half.
2. Cut out a semi-circle from the side of the box.

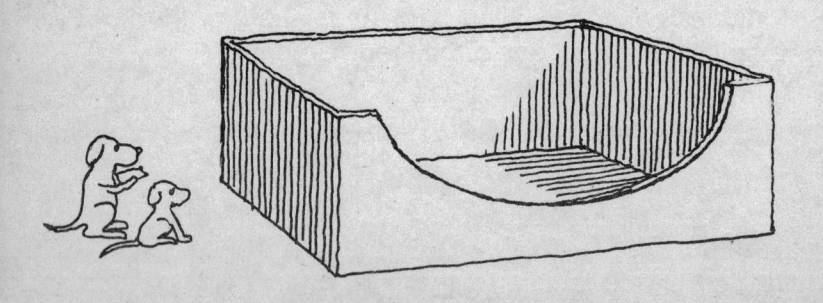

3. Tear up the newspaper and paste it all over the box.
4. When the paste is dry, paint the box any colour you like.
5. Write the name of your pet on the front of the basket.
6. Leave the box to dry out thoroughly before giving it two coats of varnish.

☆☆
PICNIC BASKET

If the children want to have a picnic with their teddy bears, here's how to make a basket to carry all the goodies in.

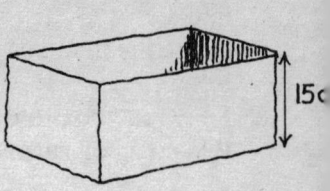

15c

What You Need:
Two small boxes, one just slightly larger than the other so they fit snugly inside each other; glue; wallpaper paste; fancy wrapping paper or wallpaper.

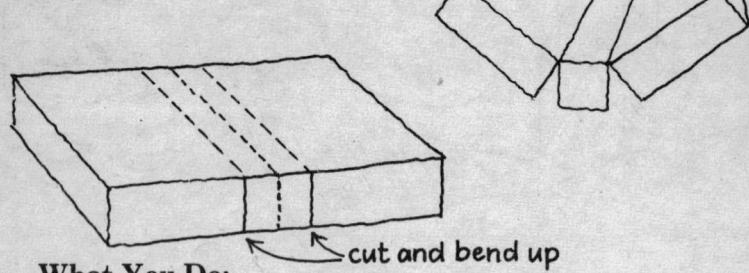

cut and bend up

What You Do:
1. Cut the smaller of the two boxes down to about 15cm.
2. To make the lid, cut the side off the larger box leaving an edge of about 4cm all round. Draw a line across the centre of the lid, then mark 2cm each side of the line and draw lines across.
3. Cut up the two lines on each side of the lid and glue it on to the picnic basket by the two centre pieces.

4. From the other piece of the large box, cut a section of card 4cm wide. Fit it on to the picnic basket to make a handle. Glue it in place.
5. Finally, cover the box inside and out with pretty paper.

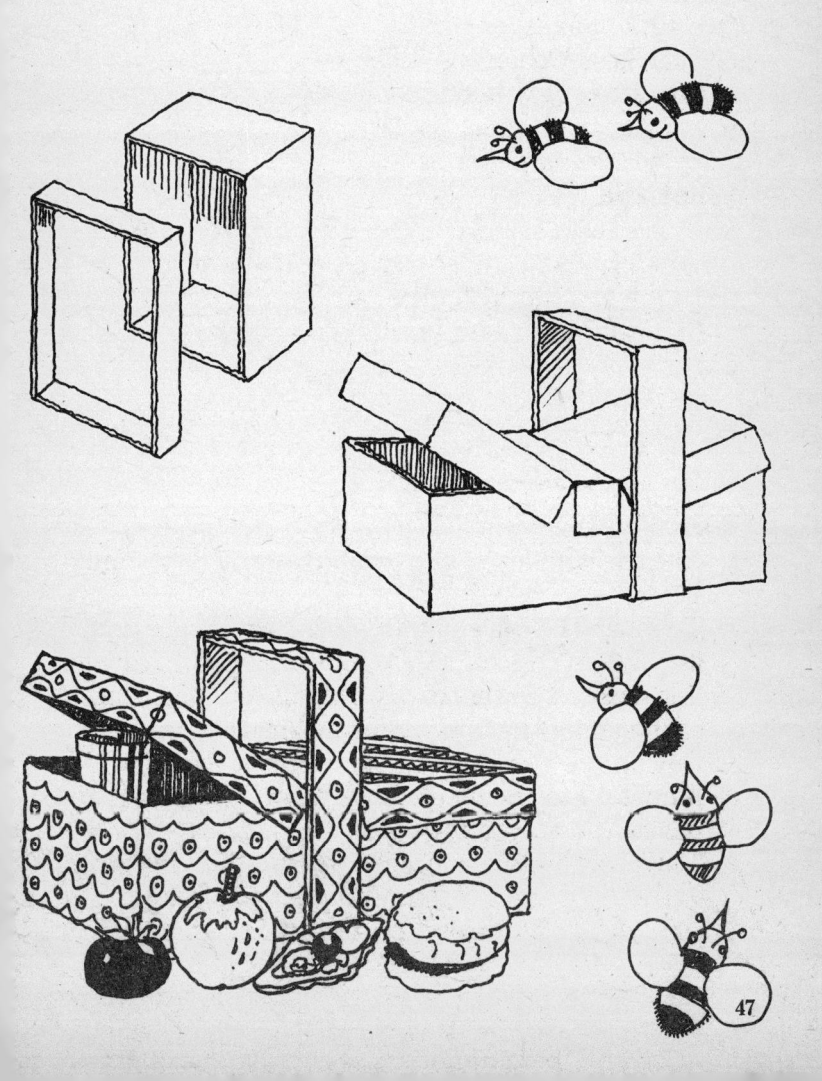

PIN BALL MACHINE

You and your kids can be pinball wizards with this super pinball machine.

What You Need:
One medium sized cardboard box; five marbles or small balls; glue; sticky tape; a sheet of stiff paper; a kitchen roll tube; a piece of dowel about 3cm in diameter and about 12cm long.

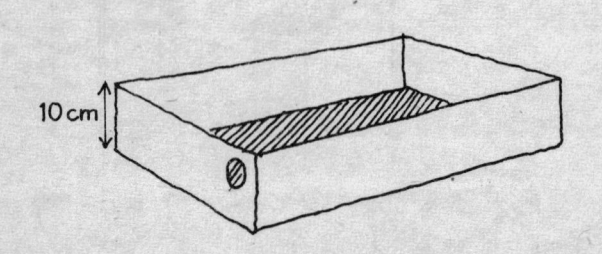

What You Do:
1. Cut one side off the box leaving approximately a 10cm edge all the way round to form a tray. Cut a hole about 3cm in diameter in the top corner of one end.

2. From the remaining part of the box cut out a rectangle that just fits inside the tray. Bend one end up to make a lip about 6cm high and cut a hole 3cm in diameter in the right hand corner. Cut five holes the same diameter as the kitchen roll tube in the other part of the rectangle.

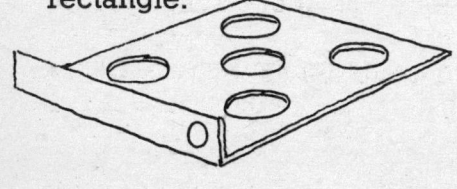

3. Cut the kitchen roll tube into five equal lengths and tape or glue them in the holes, making sure they do not stick above the surface.

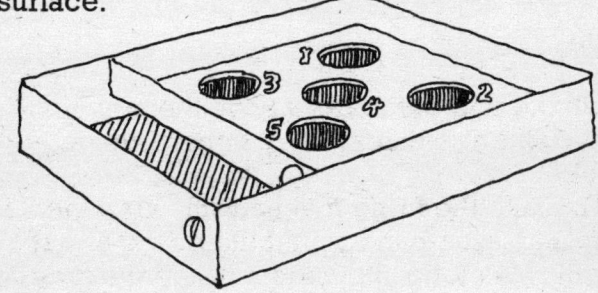

4. Glue the whole thing into the bottom tray.
5. Mark the numbers 1–5 next to the holes.

6. Roll the stiff paper into a tube (check that it is just wide enough to fit into the 3cm holes and that it is at least 9cm long) and tape along the edge.
7. Cut a section out of the tube as shown and slide it through the two 3cm holes. With the scissors make four cuts about 2 cm deep in the end of the tube.
8. Fold back the flaps and glue the tube into place as shown.

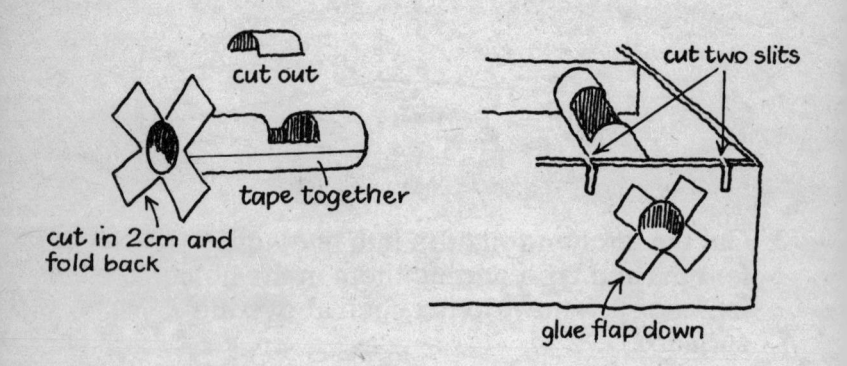

cut out

tape together

cut in 2cm and fold back

cut two slits

glue flap down

9. On the end of the tray above the tube, cut two slits about 2cm deep either side of the tube.
10. To make the firing mechanism, wrap the small elastic band round the dowel about half-way along and slide it inside the tube till it is stopped by the elastic.

    Loop the thick elastic band into the two slits and round the end of the dowel.

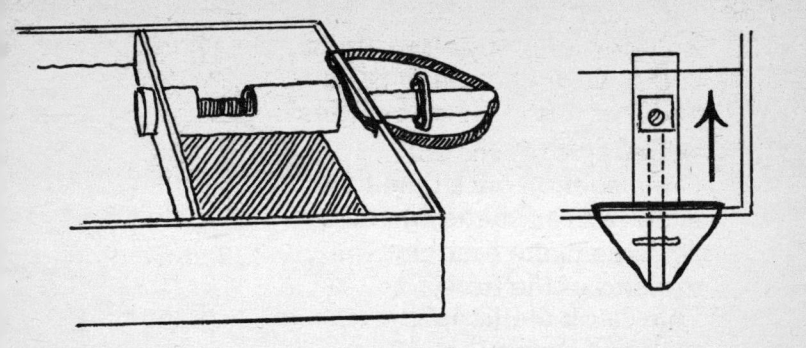

11. Drop a marble into the hole in the tube, pull the dowel back and fire away!

POSTBOX

Children love to send and receive letters. I think that it's a good idea to encourage them to write letters from early on. This fun postbox will do just that. When it's made they will be able to write letters to each other and post them. It's an excellent way to teach them how to read and write each other's names and addresses.

What You Need:
One tall medium sized box; red paint; sellotape.

What You Do:
1. Close up the flaps and sellotape them shut.
2. Cut a rectangle about 5cm by 15cm out of the front of the box.
3. Make a flap at the bottom for the postman to collect the letters. Just cut along the bottom then up each side about 15cm.

4. Finally paint the whole box bright red.
   While it's drying, get busy writing some letters and postcards.

☆☆☆ PUNCH & JUDY PUPPET THEATRE

I'm sure you will agree with me when I say that all children love a Punch and Judy show. Usually the shows are at the seaside, but now I will show you how to make a Punch and Judy theatre so the kids can have a show whenever they want.

What You Need:

One very large box, the bigger the better (I used one that a fridge came packed in); some material to make the curtains; a piece of cane or dowel a little longer than the width of the box; paint; craft knife; glue; ruler; pencil.

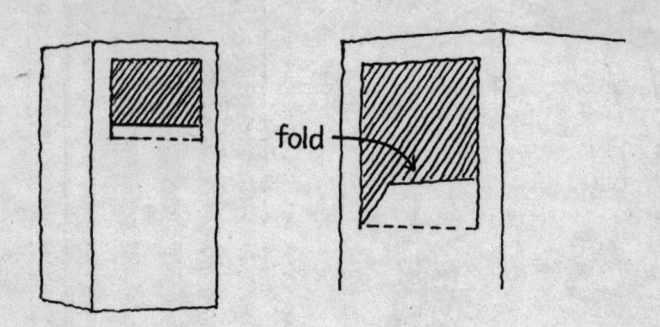

What You Do:
1. Trim the flaps off the box.
2. Mark out a square on the front of the box as shown in the drawing and cut it out with a craft knife.

make holes either side

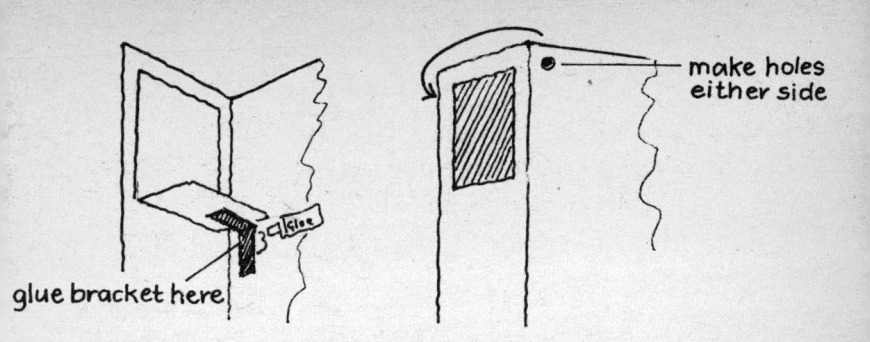

glue bracket here

3. Make two 12cm cuts straight down from the bottom corners of the square and bend the flap inwards to make a shelf.
4. Cut out two rectangles of card about 15cm by 15cm and bend them into an 'L' shape. Glue one either end of the shelf to form a support.
5. Pierce a hole either side of the box.
6. Cut half-way up both sides of the box at the back, then cut across and remove the section. This is the entrance to the theatre.

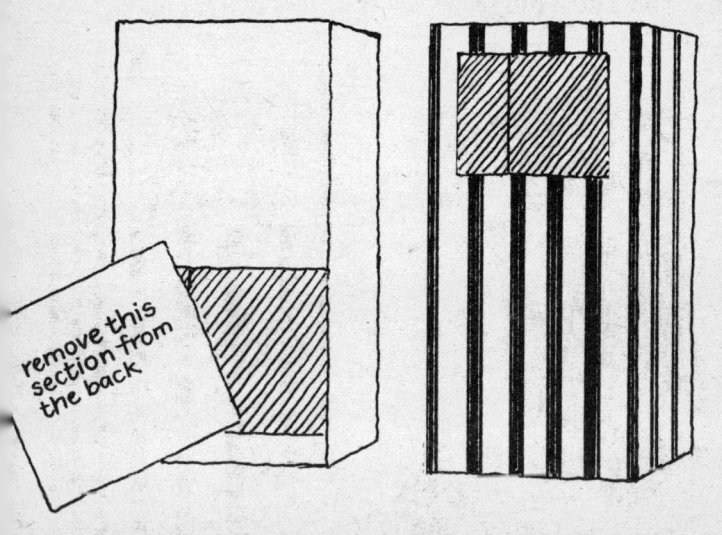

remove this section from the back

7. Now paint the box bright colours. I used red and yellow stripes.

8. While the paint is drying, cut the material into two pieces big enough to make a pair of curtains. Fold over about 5cm at the top and glue down.

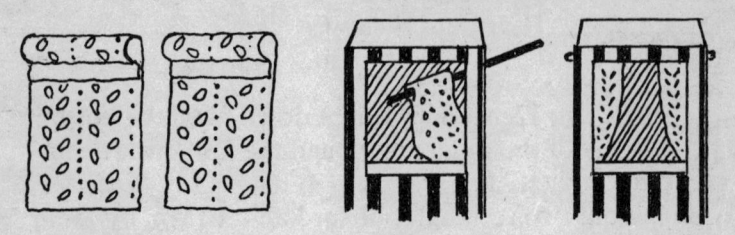

9. Push the dowel into one side of the box. Then slide the curtains on and push the other end of the dowel into the other hole.

You can now put on a show using the traditional Punch and Judy Puppets, or make up your own plays using ordinary glove puppets.

SERVICE STATION

Toy cars are a lot of fun, but they are even more fun if they have a place to drive in and out of. Here is a service station that's quick and easy to make. It is also a useful place to keep the cars when they are not being played with.

What You Need:
One small flatish box; two kitchen roll tubes; paint; two or three empty matchboxes; sellotape; glue.

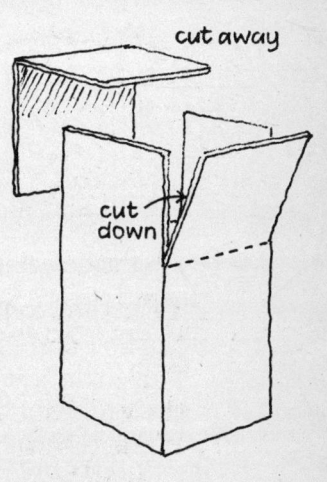

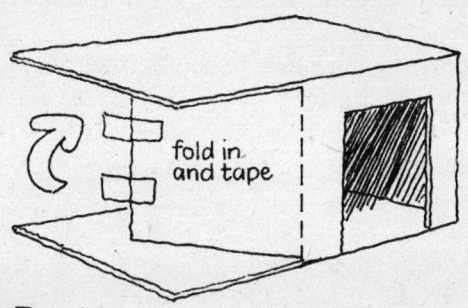

What You Do:
1. Measure half-way down the box and draw a line all the way round.
2. Cut away the top and half of one side.
3. Cut half-way down the other side. Fold the side in and tape it in place.
4. Cut out a doorway on the side.

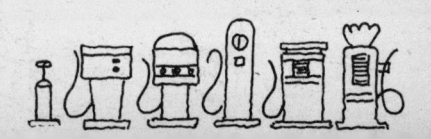

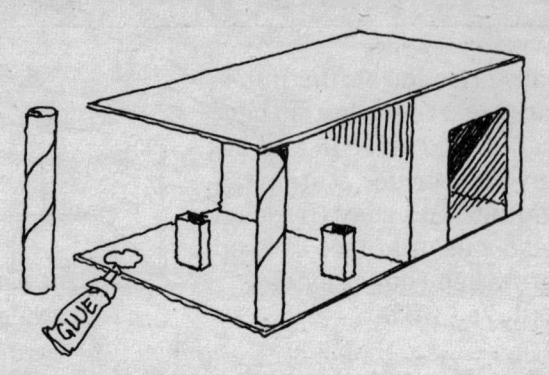

5. Trim the kitchen roll tubes so they fit in between the box and glue them in each corner.
6. Paint the service station. Use bright colours for the walls and paint the floor and roof dark grey.
7. While the station is drying, paint the matchboxes white like petrol pumps, then glue them in place.

Once the toy cars are added the whole thing will look very realistic.

SHIP

A child's imagination will turn this easy-to-make ship into an ocean-going liner. If you can find big enough boxes, two children can sit inside and sail the seven seas together.

What You Need:
Two large boxes, the bigger the better; one small sturdy box as a seat.

What You Do:
1. Cut the bottom and top completely out of one of the boxes.
2. Bend the box down the centre to make the bow and stern of the boat.
3. Trim the flaps off the second box and cut the shape of the cabin out. Cut a circle out of each side for the port holes.

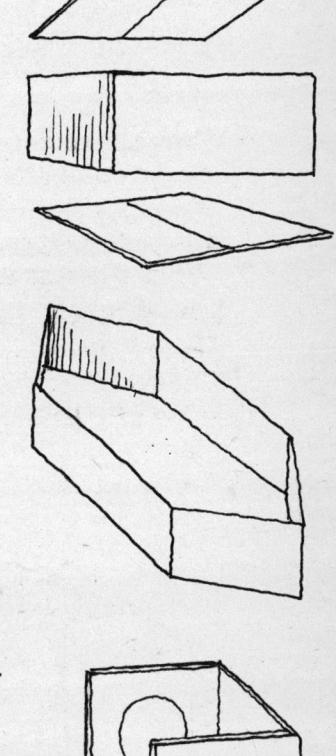

4. Place the cabin inside the hull and tape it in place.
5. Place the small box inside the cabin to sit on.

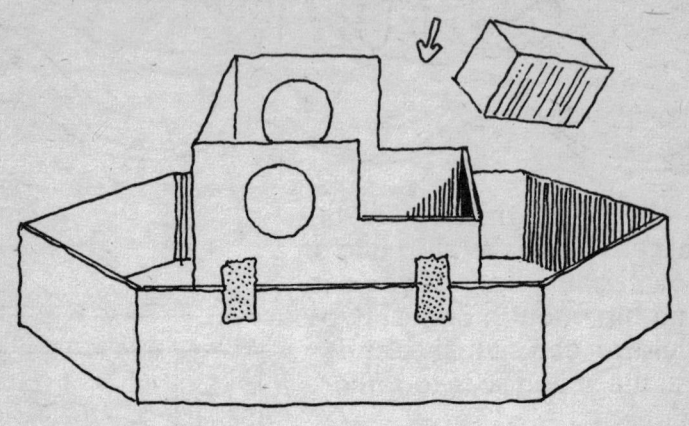

6. Make the ship's wheel by cutting a circle from cardboard. Cut a hole in the centre of the wheel just big enough to push the kitchen roll tube through. Draw spokes on the wheel to make it look realistic.
7. Cut another hole in the front of the cabin the same size as the tube and secure the wheel in place with tape.
8. Paint and decorate the ship.

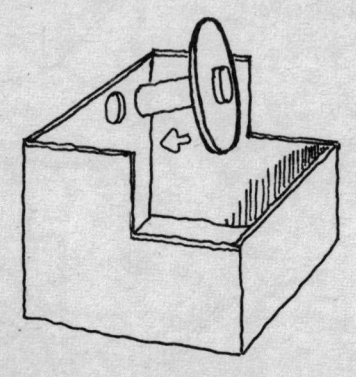

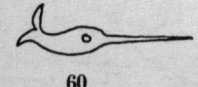

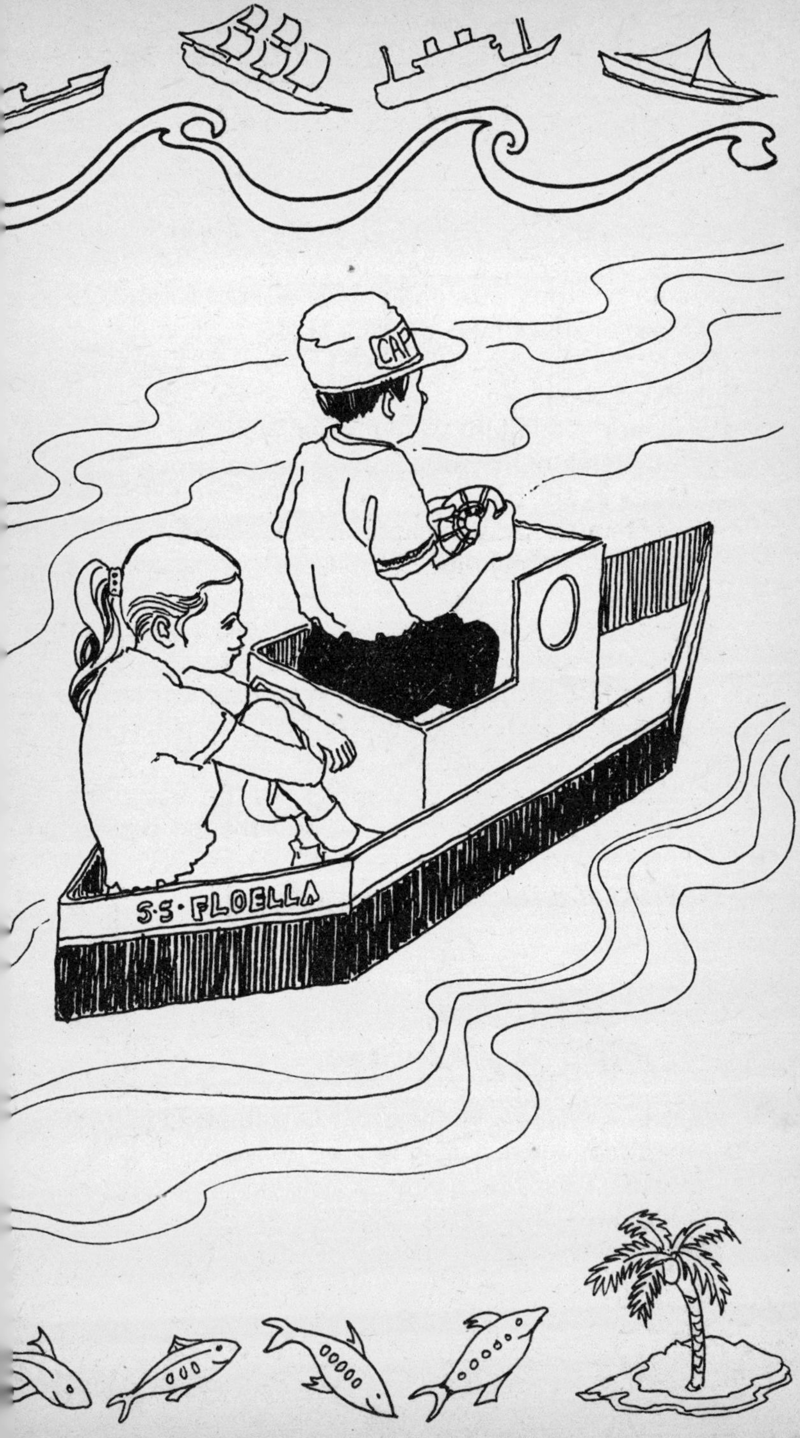
CAP
S.S. FLOELLA

SOFA

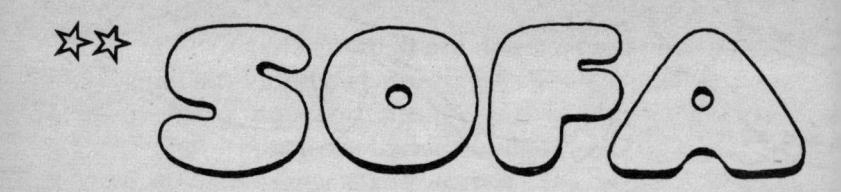

This sofa is strong enough for little ones to sit on. You'll be surprised how sturdy it is.

What You Need:
Four identical medium sized narrow boxes for the arms and back of the sofa, and one large strong flatish box as the base; craft knife; a roll of old unwanted patterned wallpaper; wallpaper paste; pencil; brown parcel tape.

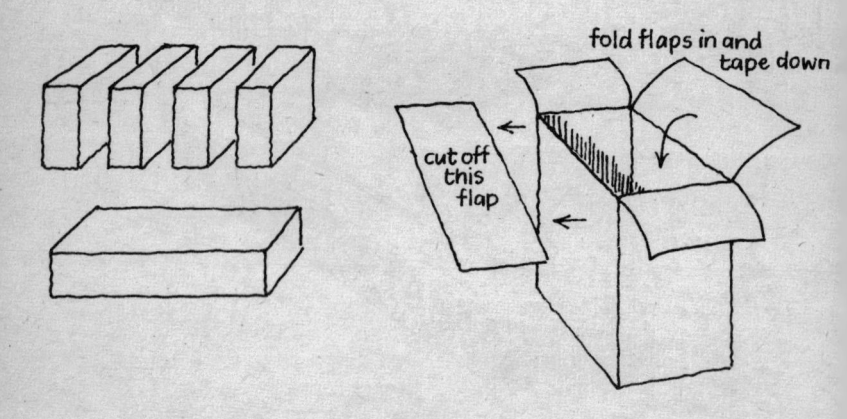

What You Do:
1. Trim one of the long flaps off each of the narrow boxes, then push all the other flaps inside and tape them down, This gives the boxes extra strength.
2. Fold all the flaps of the large box inside and tape them down.

3. Arrange the boxes on the floor, as shown in the drawing, making sure the sides without the flaps are facing inwards and mark the height of the base on the arms and back of the sofa.
4. On the side of the narrow boxes where there is no flap, measure in about 7cm from each edge and cut a line up to the mark you have just made.
5. Cut a slit along the very edge of one long side and both short sides of the base and slot the arms and back in as shown.

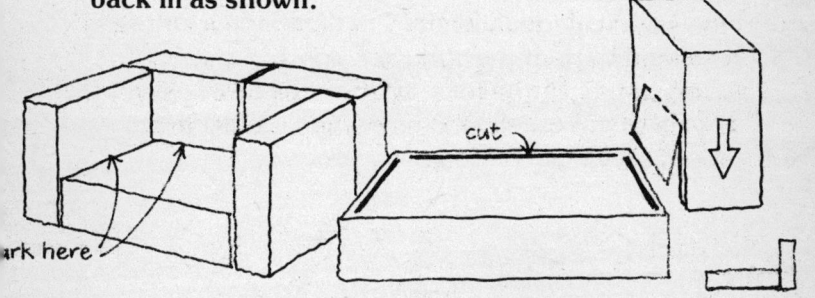

6. Finally cut the wallpaper into large pieces and paste them all over the sofa.

SPACE STATION

This super space station looks good hanging from the ceiling in a child's bedroom as a sci-fi mobile, or it can be used as a base for all those space figures children love these days.

What You Need:
One small box; four empty plastic lemonade bottles; an assortment of yoghurt containers; drinking straws; foil cake-tins; bottle tops; kitchen roll tubes; silver foil and polystyrene packing etc; white emulsion paint; strong glue.

What You Do:
1. Tape the flaps of the box shut.
2. Paint the four bottles and the box white and put them aside to dry.
3. Cut a small hole in all four sides of the box, just big enough to push the bottle tops into. Glue the bottles in place.

4. Stick bottle tops and yoghurt containers all over the space station. Use straws as aerials and foil cake dishes as radar scanners. You can really go mad and use as much imagination as you like.

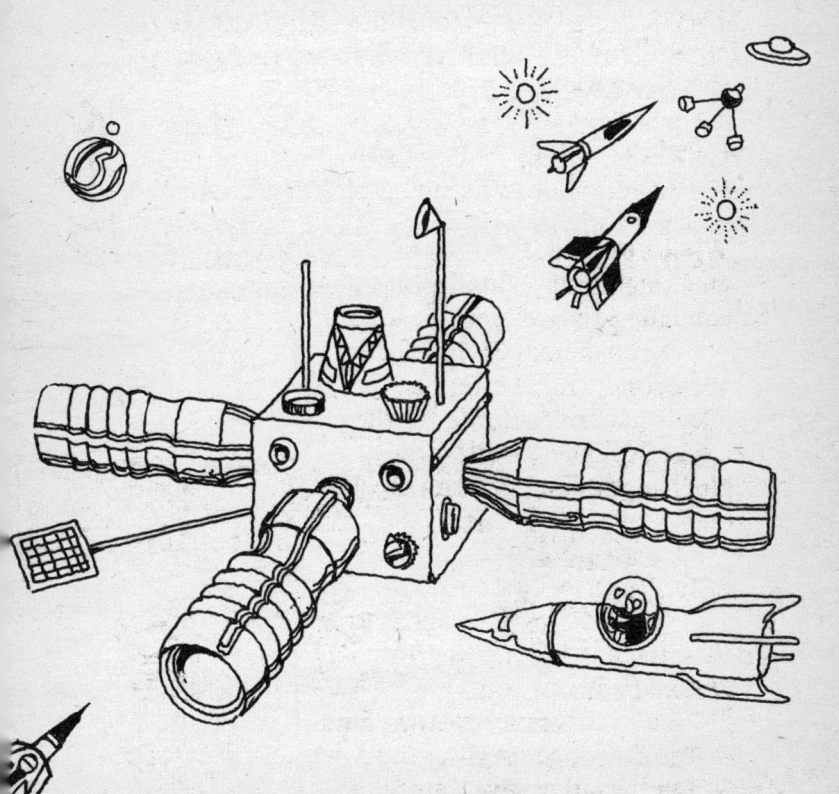

5. Space craft and space stations are always painted white in sci-fi films so I suggest you do the same. When you are satisfied with the result, use strong thread or fishing line to hang the space station from the ceiling. It looks great.

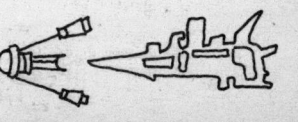

✭✭
SPACE SUIT

This is my son Aston's favourite. He really feels as if he's a spaceman when he's got it on. He always insists I make one for his friends when they come to visit. It's a real winner!

What You Need:
One small square box just big enough to fit over your head; an oblong box about 25cm wide by 40cm long; craft knife; one plastic lemonade bottle for the oxygen cylinder; white paint; glue; sticky tape; brown parcel tape.

What You Do:
1. Trim the two side flaps off the small box leaving the front and back ones on.
2. Mark out a hole as shown in the drawing and cut it out.
3. On the larger box, carefully mark out the sides as shown in the drawing and cut away. Do the same with the top. Check to see if the box will fit comfortably over the shoulders of the person who is to wear the spacesuit. Trim if necessary.

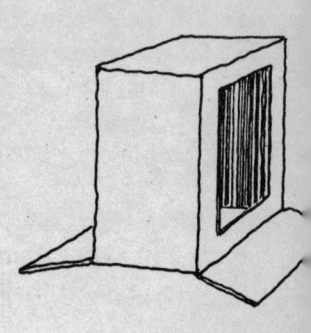

4. Use parcel tape to fix the small box on to the top of the larger one, making sure that the flap at the back is on the outside.
5. Paint the suit white.
6. Next hold the lemonade bottle against the back of the spacesuit and mark out where the bottle cap touches the underside of the flap. Cut a hole in it just big enough for the bottle top to fit tightly in.
7. Push the top of the bottle into the hole and then use sticky tape to secure the bottle to the box.
8. If you want, you can decorate the suit with bottle tops as buttons and dials.

✰✰ SUITCASE

Kids will love this suitcase to pack their clothes in when they are pretending to go away on holiday.

What You Need:
Two boxes that fit one inside the other very tightly; wide parcel tape; glue; brown paint.

What You Do:
1. Trim the smaller of the two boxes down to about 20cm in depth.
2. Do the same with the larger one to about 10cm in depth.
3. Place the boxes side by side and tape them together, using plenty of tape as shown in the drawing.
4. Close the boxes and tape along the outside.
5. From a scrap piece of cardboard cut out two handle shapes. Make them about 14cm wide by 14cm deep and fold them as shown.

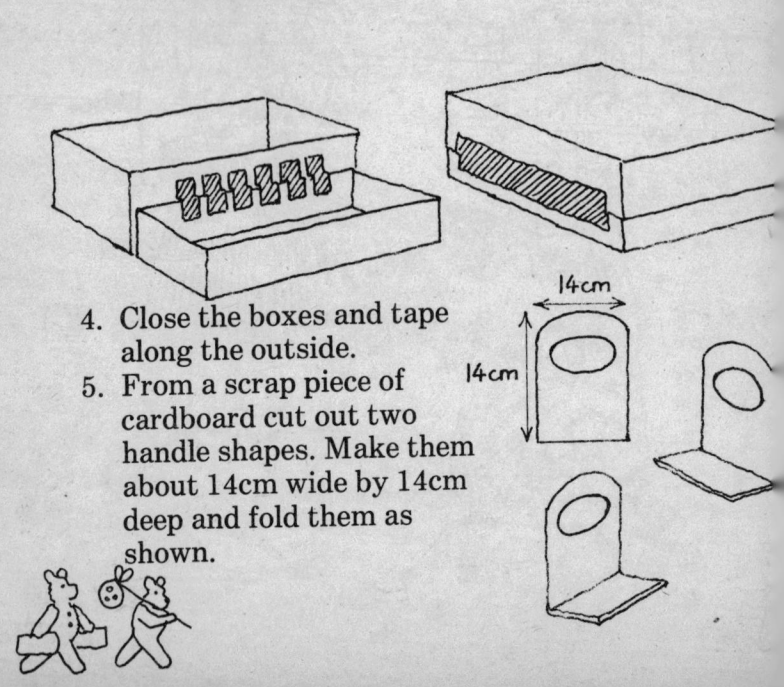

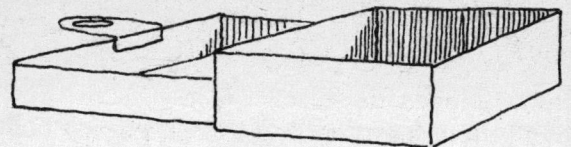

6. Glue one handle inside the lid of the suitcase as shown.
7. Close the lid and where the handle meets the base, cut a slit about 15cm long.

cut slit here

8. Slot the other handle through the slit from the inside and glue in place. Now when you close the case both sides of the handle should meet and when you grip them together the case will be held shut.
9. Finally, paint the suitcase.

TABLE

This table is great for a toy's tea party.

What You Need:
One large box; poster paint; craft knife; pencil; ruler.

What You Do:
1. Trim the flaps off the box.
2. Mark 5cm from the side and top edges of the box and draw lines as shown in the diagram.
3. Cut along the lines
4. Paint the table.

TELEVISION

Do your children wish they could be on television? Well here's the answer, their very own television set!

What You Need:
One medium sized box; two or three bottle tops; some corrugated paper; craft knife; glue; black and brown paint.

What You do:
1. Trim the flaps off the box, then mark out the screen on one side. Make sure the screen is slightly to one side so there is room to fit on the controls and the speaker. Paint the front brown.
2. To make the speaker grille, cut out an oblong shape from the corrugated paper, just big enough to fit beside the screen. Paint it black.
3. When the paint is dry, glue the speaker grille on to the front of the television.
4. Glue the bottle tops underneath the speaker grille.
5. If you want, you can paint the inside of the television either a plain colour or with a 'set' like the news room. Then someone can kneel behind a table and put the television over their head and read the news.

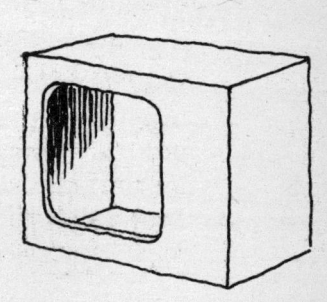

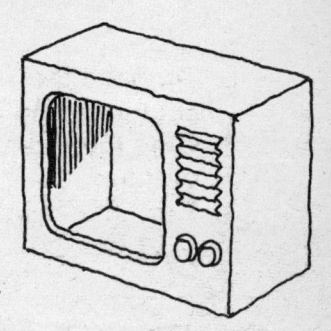

TRAIN

What You Need:
Four empty cereal boxes; string; glue; paint; scissors.

What You Do:
1. Measure a line around each box about 9cm up from the bottom and cut around. These are the carriages and the engine.

2. To make the wheels, cut out 18 circles about 4cm in diameter.
3. Glue four on each carriage and six on the engine.
4. Paint the carriages and the engine.

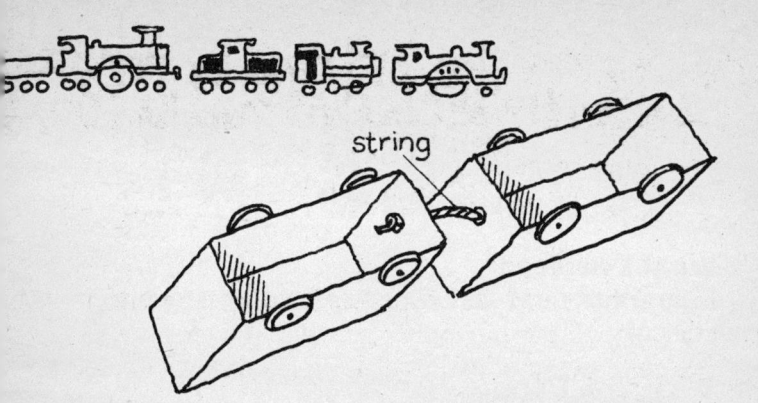

5. Pierce a hole at the end of each carriage and at the back of the engine; thread a short piece of string through and tie a knot in each end.

WASHING MACHINE

This washing machine will come in very useful on wash day for washing the toys' clothes.

What You Need:
One large box; craft knife; plastic jar top; cling film; sticky tape; glue; white paint; pencil; a dinner plate and a side plate; scrap of cardboard.

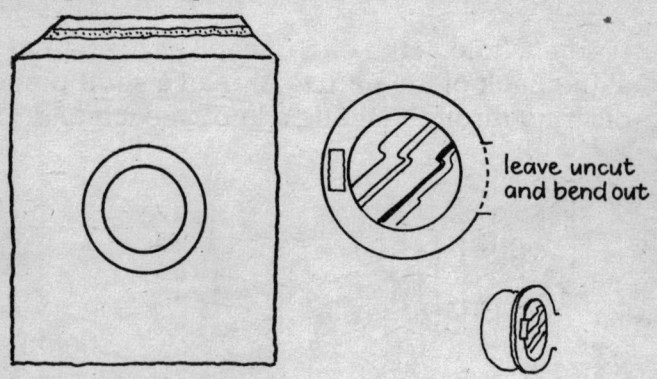

leave uncut and bend out

What You Do:
1. Close up the top of the box and tape shut.
2. On the front of the box mark a large circle by drawing round the dinner plate, then mark a smaller circle inside using the side plate.
3. With the craft knife, cut out the inner circle, then cut most of the way round the outer one. Just leave a bit about 5cm uncut at the side as a hinge. Bend the door outwards.

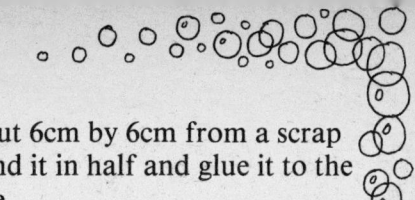

4. Cut a small square about 6cm by 6cm from a scrap piece of cardboard, bend it in half and glue it to the door opposite the hinge.
5. Paint the box white.
6. Tape a piece of cling film across the inside of the door.
7. Glue the plastic jar top on the front of the washing machine above the door.

Wendy House

It's so nice to have a secret little place to hide away in. Kids love to hide inside their own little house where their imaginations can run wild. If you can get hold of a huge box, the type that a freezer or a washing machine is packed in, then here's how to make a great house with it.

What You Need:
One very large box; one medium sized box; two small boxes; strong parcel tape; paint; curtain material; an empty plastic lemonade bottle.

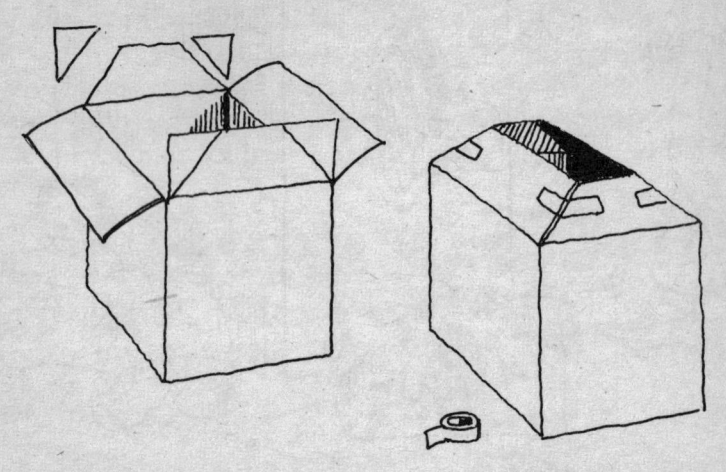

What You Do:
1. Open up the flaps on the big box and cut off the corners of the end ones.
2. Tape the long flaps to the edges of the short ones to form part of the roof.

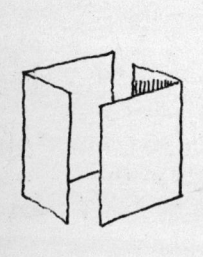

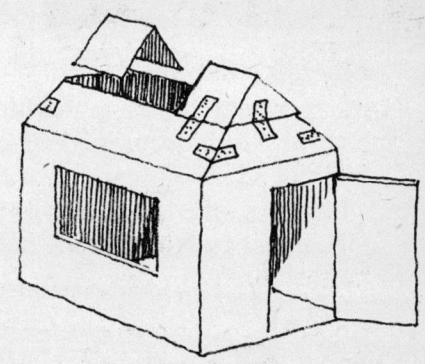

3. Cut the medium sized box diagonally into two halves and tape them in place to form the rest of the roof.
4. Cut out a door so that it hinges along one edge of the box and cut a window out of the side.
5. In one of the small boxes cut a hole large enough for the lemonade bottle to be pushed through. Tape the bottle in place and put the assembled chimney on top of the house.

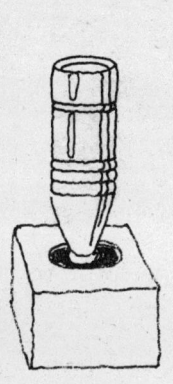

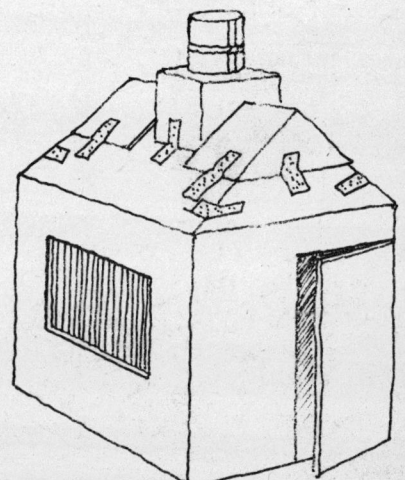

6. Tape the other small box to the outside of the window as a window box.
7. Paint the roof like tiles and the walls like bricks.

Make some curtains and put some plastic flowers in the window box.

Well, there we are – lots of amazing things to make from cardboard boxes!

I hope the ideas in this book have given both parents and kids hours of fun. I certainly had fun thinking them up.

I am sure you all will have lots of ideas of your own now and won't be able to resist making something whenever you see an empty cardboard box . . . I can't.

Love and hugs

Floella.